"I hereby dedicate this book to every young Indian working professional striving to break free from the middle-class trap; I would love to share this knowledge with you, because I have walked your path."

HOW TO BUILD YOUR BEST LIFE BY 40

THE ULTIMATE BLUEPRINT FOR SUCCESS, WEALTH & FULFILMENT

DR. SAPTARSHI SANKAR CHAKRABARTI (PHD)

Contents

The Author's Bio

Dr. SAPTARSHI SANKAR CHAKRABARTI

Driven by a deep-rooted passion for authorship and knowledge sharing, Dr. Saptarshi Sankar Chakrabarti is an accomplished architect, serial entrepreneur, and strategic mentor with over two decades of experience in India and abroad. Specializing in large-scale urban development, smart cities, sustainable tourism destinations, and mega-infrastructure projects, his mastery in architectural project management—especially the use of Work Breakdown Structures, Automated Systems, and Trackable Processes—uniquely positions him as a visionary leader in both professional and financial realms.

For the first time ever, Dr. Chakrabarti has innovatively applied these robust principles of architectural planning and systematic project management to the domains of personal finance and wealth-building. By transforming complex financial strategies into clear, structured, and actionable blueprints, he empowers young Indian working professionals to break free from financial struggles, build sustainable wealth, and create a life of lasting success and personal freedom—with the precision, clarity, and elegance of an architectural masterpiece.

He can be reached through:

- Mobile/WhatsApp: +91 9477586654
- Email: sschakrabarti@gmail.com
- LinkedIn: https://www.linkedin.com/in/saptarshischakrabarti
- Facebook: https://www.facebook.com/sschakrabarti.fanpage
- YouTube: https://www.youtube.com/saptarshichakrabarti
- Instagram: https://www.instagram.com/architectsaptarshi
- Twitter: https://www.twitter.com/ss_chakrabarti

Acknowledgements

I would like to express my deepest gratitude to my wife, whose unwavering love and support have been the foundation of everything I have achieved. To my beloved daughter, whose future in these challenging and rapidly changing times has been my greatest motivation to write this book—may the lessons I have learned guide not only you, but every young Indian striving to break free from the middle-class trap, just as I have done myself, learning everything the hard way. A heartfelt thanks to everyone around me who has shaped my worldview; I consider this book a complete reflection of your wisdom, not mine. Thank you, everyone, for being part of this journey.

—The Author

Preface

Nobody is coming to save you!

If you're from a middle-class Indian family, society expects you to survive—not thrive. You are told to study hard, get a degree, land a stable job, and settle into a life of predictability. You are conditioned to believe that financial security means a steady pay check, that success is defined by promotions and increments, and that retirement is the finish line of a life well spent.

But what if I told you that this mind-set is the very reason most people remain stuck? What if I told you that this script, passed down from generation to generation, is precisely why financial and personal freedom remain out of reach for so many?

I was one of those people. I followed the script. I did what I was told. I worked hard, earned my degrees, secured a stable job, and settled into what was considered a "safe" life. Yet, despite doing everything right, I found myself caught in a cycle of stress, financial limitations, and the constant worry that one unexpected crisis could upend everything I had worked for.

So, I **decided to stop playing by the rules.**

I stopped living for job security and started working toward **financial freedom.** I questioned everything I was taught about money, success, and wealth-building. I built a system—one that took me from merely surviving to thriving. **And now, I am handing this blueprint to you.**

Why This Book? Why Now?

The world is evolving faster than ever before. Job security is fading. AI and automation are eliminating traditional career paths. The cost of living is rising, while salary growth stagnates. Inflation erodes savings faster than most people realize. **The old formula—study, work, save, retire—simply doesn't work anymore.**

The only way to thrive in this new economy is to take control of your financial future—before it's too late.

This book is not about get-rich-quick schemes. It's not about extreme frugality. It's about **understanding money as a tool**, mastering high-income skills, investing early, designing multiple income streams, and using **time as leverage** for wealth creation.

By following this step-by-step approach, you will be able to:

- Escape the paycheck-to-paycheck cycle and build **true financial security.**
- Develop **high-income skills** that ensure long-term career stability.
- Invest smartly in **assets that generate passive income.**
- Create **multiple revenue streams** so that money continues to flow in—even when you're not actively working.
- Achieve **financial freedom before 40**—so you can focus on what truly matters.

This book is not just a collection of ideas—it's an **actionable framework** backed by real-world execution.

The Middle-Class Trap: What Nobody Tells

You

For decades, the Indian middle-class has been trapped in **a cycle of survival.**

- Work hard, but never make enough to stop worrying.
- Save money, but inflation erodes its value.
- Invest cautiously, but never in high-return assets.
- Rely on a job, but fear layoffs and economic downturns.

Most people **spend their entire lives in financial uncertainty**, never realizing that money should be working for them—not the other way around.

If you're tired of this cycle, it's time to change the way you think about success.

How My Education as an Architect Shaped My Perspective

Unlike conventional career paths, my **primary skill education as an architect** gave me a unique perspective on financial independence, structured planning, and execution. Architecture is not just about designing buildings; it is about **understanding systems, visualizing the bigger picture, and breaking down complex projects into executable steps.** These very skills became the foundation of my wealth-building mind-set.

Architecture taught me to think in phases—starting with an idea, refining the blueprint, implementing it step by step, and finally, executing it into a real-world structure. I realized that financial independence, business growth, and wealth creation follow the same **structured** process. **You cannot build financial freedom without a blueprint.**

More importantly, my architectural education **inculcated an entrepreneurial mind-set** in me. Unlike traditional jobs where you are trained to work within a system, architecture forces you to think like a **problem solver, an innovator, and a strategist.** You must balance **creativity with practicality, resources with execution, and long-term sustainability with immediate action.** This same mind-set applies to business, investments, and financial planning.

This is why **architects, doctors, lawyers, and chartered accountants** are among the few professions where signatures carry monetary value. But this book is not just about choosing a profession—it is about designing a **life where wealth works for you, not against you.**

The Blueprint for Financial Freedom Before 40

This book is not about theories—it's about **action.**

It follows a **six-phase approach,** each aligned with critical stages of life, from early childhood to financial independence. Each chapter provides practical steps to build a strong financial foundation, maximize income, scale investments, and create long-term generational wealth.

- **Ages 0–5:** Early Parenting and Financial Awareness
- **Ages 5–12:** Building Core Values and Financial Literacy
- **Ages 12–19:** Cultivating a Wealth Mindset and Escaping Middle-Class Traps
- **Ages 19–26:** Mastering Career, Finances, and Relationships
- **Ages 26–33:** Maximizing Earnings, Accelerating Wealth Creation, and Building Family Foundations

- **Ages 33–40**: Securing Financial Independence, Time Freedom, and Creating Legacy

By following this roadmap, by 40, you should have **multiple income streams, investments that grow while you sleep, and a life that gives you time freedom**—not just financial stability, but actual **independence.**

The First Step Begins Here

The biggest regret most people have is **wishing they had started earlier.**

Financial freedom isn't built overnight, but **every day you wait is a day lost.** The earlier you start, the easier it is to break free.

This book is the **guide I wish I had when I started.** Every chapter, every strategy, and every principle inside it has been tested, refined, and proven to work. If you commit to applying these lessons, you won't just improve your finances—you'll transform your **entire life.**

The question is not **if** financial freedom before 40 is possible.

The question is: **Are you ready to make it happen?**

Legal Disclaimer

This book is a work of nonfiction based on the author's personal experiences, research, observations, and opinions. The information, strategies, principles, and advice contained within are provided solely for educational, informational, and general guidance purposes, and should not be interpreted or relied upon as professional, financial, legal, investment, or personal advice. Readers are strongly encouraged to consult qualified professionals before taking any actions or making any decisions based on the content of this book.

While every effort has been made to ensure accuracy and reliability, the author and publisher make no representations or warranties regarding the completeness, correctness, suitability, or applicability of the contents. Any references to real individuals, companies, organizations, or specific incidents have been included solely to illustrate and enrich the content and do not imply any endorsement or affiliation unless explicitly stated.

The author and publisher expressly disclaim any and all liability, responsibility, or loss arising directly or indirectly from any use of, or reliance upon, the information contained within this book. All responsibility for personal decisions and actions rests solely with the reader.

This book is written without intent to offend, discriminate, or disparage any individual, family, group, caste, community, creed, religion, profession, or organization. Any resemblance or reference to real persons, entities, or situations is purely illustrative and should not be taken as factual representation. Readers must exercise their own judgment and discretion when interpreting and applying the book's contents, and professional advice should always be sought for real-world situations.

Prologue

The Journey from Struggle to Freedom

I come from a middle-class working Indian family, where financial struggles were normal, and long-term wealth was never discussed. Like many others, I was taught to focus on getting a stable job, paying bills, and saving just enough to survive. But nobody ever told me how to create a life beyond this cycle. Nobody taught me how to build real wealth, how to make money work for me, or how to live a life of purpose and fulfilment. So I had to figure it all out—the hard way.

I learned, I failed, I adapted, and eventually, I built my own system for success. This book is the roadmap I wish someone had given me when I started. And now, I'm sharing it with you.

For years, I watched my family and peers struggle, always working hard but never really moving ahead. The traditional middle-class mind-set teaches us to play it safe—to get a degree, find a secure job, and hold on to it for decades. But I realized that this approach doesn't create financial independence; it creates financial dependency.

Security is not freedom. Stability is not success. Hard work without the right strategy only leads to exhaustion, not wealth.

My own transformation began with a simple yet powerful realization: **wealth is not just about earning more; it's about thinking differently.**

Breaking the Cycle: My Architectural

Perspective

As an architect by profession, I was trained to see the world differently. Architecture is about more than buildings—it's about structured thinking, visualization, and execution. Every successful project starts with a well-designed blueprint, a strong foundation, and a step-by-step execution plan. Without these, even the most ambitious projects collapse.

It was this mind-set that shaped my approach to financial independence. I realized that just like in architecture, financial freedom requires:

- **A solid foundation** – Learning high-income skills and financial literacy.
- **A clear blueprint** – Understanding investments, business strategies, and wealth multiplication.
- **Systematic execution** – Implementing a step-by-step action plan that leads to independence.

I stopped seeing money as just "income" and started seeing it as **a tool for designing my future**. Instead of working for money, I learned how to **make money work for me**. And that's when everything changed.

What This Book Will Do for You

This book is not another generic self-help guide. It's **a step-by-step roadmap** for anyone looking to escape financial uncertainty and build a life of true wealth.

It's for you if:

- You feel trapped in the paycheck-to-paycheck cycle and

want financial security.

- You're ambitious but feel stuck in the traditional job system.
- You want to build multiple streams of income without waiting until retirement.
- You're ready to take control of your money and create lasting wealth.

The process I followed is **replicable**. This book will give you **the blueprint**—you just have to follow it.

A Message to the Reader

I know what it feels like to wake up every morning, look at your bank balance, and wonder if your hard work will ever truly pay off. I know the frustration of seeing people around you stuck in the same cycle, following the same rules, and never really getting ahead.

I also know what it feels like to break free.

When you no longer live in fear of the next bill, the next EMI, or the next financial crisis, something incredible happens. You start making decisions based on **what excites you**, not what pays the bills. You start chasing growth, not just survival. You become the kind of person who no longer dreads Mondays but wakes up with a sense of purpose.

I want that for you.

I want you to stop looking at your salary as the only source of security. I want you to break the mind-set that keeps you trapped in a never-ending loop of earning, spending, and saving just enough to stay afloat.

Most importantly, I want you to stop postponing your dreams until retirement.

The life you want isn't something you have to wait for. It's something you can **build**, step by step, starting today.

This is not about taking reckless risks. It's about making **informed, strategic choices** that put you in control. It's about building a future where you have time for your family, space to explore your passions, and the **freedom to say no** to things that don't serve you.

The road ahead won't always be easy. But I promise you this—**it will be worth it.**

CHAPTER ONE

Ages 0–5 | Early Parenting and Financial Awareness

The first five years of a child's life are the most crucial in determining their long-term cognitive, emotional, and social development. Research suggests that 90% of a child's brain develops by the age of five, making this period critical in shaping intelligence, problem-solving abilities, emotional resilience, and habits that last a lifetime (Centre on the Developing Child, Harvard University). For middle-class Indian parents, this phase presents both an opportunity and a challenge—balancing work, financial stability, and the demanding task of raising a well-rounded child.

Who?

This chapter is for young couples and parents who are raising children in Indian middle-class households. Whether you live in an urban city with access to premium preschools or a small town where traditional family values dominate, the principles of early childhood development remain universal. Every parent wants the best for their child, but without the right knowledge and tools, they often rely on outdated practices, excessive screen time, or passive learning environments. This chapter provides a structured approach to laying a solid foundation for lifelong success.

Why?

A child's early years dictate their lifelong approach to learning, emotional stability, and overall personality. The environments they are exposed to, the habits they cultivate, and the emotional security they receive influence their ability to handle relationships, careers, and financial independence in the future. Scientific research has demonstrated that early experiences impact brain architecture, affecting everything from memory retention to emotional intelligence (National Scientific Council on the Developing Child). Parents who actively engage in structured, evidence-based early education strategies provide their children with a distinct advantage in life.

What?

Raising a child is not just about feeding, clothing, and ensuring their physical safety. It is about equipping them with fundamental skills such as independence, self-awareness, and emotional regulation. In a middle-class Indian household, where education is often considered the gateway to success, it is crucial to emphasize that formal schooling alone is not enough. Real learning begins at home, with parents as the primary educators. This means:

- Teaching children to take care of themselves through simple tasks like dressing, eating independently, and maintaining hygiene.
- Introducing foundational learning concepts through storytelling, interactive play, and hands-on activities.
- Helping children develop emotional intelligence by understanding feelings, managing frustration, and learning self-discipline.

Where?

Early childhood education primarily happens at home, with complementary experiences from preschool, outdoor play, and cultural exposure. Indian families traditionally emphasize family bonding, with grandparents playing an active role in upbringing. While this offers emotional security, it is essential for parents to ensure that children are also exposed to structured educational experiences that nurture curiosity and problem-solving abilities. Playschools and day-cares can provide social interaction opportunities, but the primary learning environment must be a child's home.

When?

The first five years are divided into different phases:

- **0–2 years:** Sensory exploration, developing a bond with caregivers, understanding basic words, and emotional security.
- **2–3 years:** Increased independence, learning self-help skills, understanding routines, and early

communication.

- **3–5 years:** Advanced language development, creativity, problem-solving skills, and structured play-based learning. Each stage requires specific engagement strategies from parents to maximize brain development and cognitive growth.

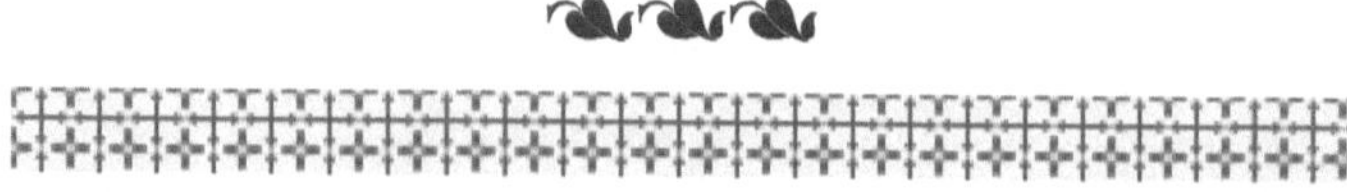

Perspective View

The first five years of a child's life are the defining moments that shape their future—their intelligence, emotional resilience, social skills, and overall success depend heavily on experiences during this critical period. Born and brought up in a middle-class Indian working family myself, I vividly recall the balance my parents constantly sought between their demanding careers and the monumental responsibility of raising a child capable of thriving in an ever-changing world. My early life experiences mirrored those of countless middle-class Indian households, where stability, academic success, and financial security were emphasized. Yet, the importance of holistic early childhood development—nurturing independence, emotional intelligence, and social awareness—often remained overlooked or undervalued in the traditional upbringing patterns I witnessed around me.

As a child, my parents, both government employees, deeply embedded in the middle-class ethos of security and stability, dedicated themselves to ensuring I had everything necessary for academic success. However, beyond structured schoolwork and disciplined routines, early cognitive development through creative play, emotional expression, and active learning experiences was not always prioritized, largely due to their lack of exposure to modern developmental insights. This was not unusual in my surroundings—most Indian parents of that generation believed that formal schooling and disciplined routines were sufficient foundations for lifelong achievement.

It was only much later, during my professional education as an architect, that I realized how crucial these early years truly were in shaping holistic thinking, creative problem-solving, and emotional maturity. Architecture taught me the invaluable lesson of foundational strength—every grand building, every successful project starts with meticulous planning, design, and a strong base. Reflecting on this, I understood how early childhood development mirrors the architectural principles I learned. Just as no building can sustain itself without a robust foundation, no individual can attain their fullest potential without a well-nurtured, balanced upbringing from their earliest days.

Scientific research from institutions like Harvard University's Centre on the Developing Child reinforces this critical truth: 90% of a child's brain development occurs by age five. The experiences and stimuli provided during this time significantly affect their future capabilities, including memory retention, language skills, social interactions, and emotional stability. Thus, for every middle-class Indian parent, these initial years must become a conscious period of structured nurturing, not simply passive caretaking or an over-reliance on external educational institutions.

Effective early parenting is much more than ensuring physical well-being; it's about fostering self-sufficiency and emotional stability. From personal experience, I understand how even seemingly trivial activities, such as allowing children to pick their clothes, eat independently, or perform basic self-care tasks, contribute significantly to their confidence and decision-making skills. In traditional Indian households, where grandparents or extended family members often assist in childcare, children may become overly dependent and lack initiative. While this extended support is a comforting and valuable aspect of our culture, parents must consciously incorporate activities to develop personal responsibility and autonomy early on.

Interactive play and hands-on learning experiences offer profound developmental advantages compared to conventional rote-learning practices prevalent in many Indian homes. Early in my parenting journey, influenced by my architectural training, I incorporated creative play—storytelling, sensory explorations, and rhythm-based activities—into my child's daily routine, inspired by insights from developmental experts like Dr. John Medina, author of Brain Rules for Baby. Simple Indian stories from Panchatantra or mythology, paired with hands-on exploration using materials like clay or textures like water, dramatically improved cognitive engagement, problem-solving skills, and emotional connections for my daughter. These structured yet playful learning environments allowed her to naturally absorb fundamental concepts while fostering creativity and curiosity.

Developing emotional intelligence and self-regulation early is equally crucial. Drawing parallels again from architecture, I realized that just as the structural integrity of a building depends on balanced distribution of weight and stress, emotional stability in life requires understanding feelings, managing frustrations, and cultivating self-discipline. Renowned experts like Daniel J. Siegel in The Whole-Brain Child highlight the neuroscience behind emotional regulation, asserting that early childhood emotional development profoundly influences lifelong mental health, relationships, and professional success. Practicing mindfulness techniques and empathetic communication within our family significantly enhanced emotional resilience, teaching my daughter early on how to handle disappointments, empathize with others, and manage emotional impulses constructively.

An integral part of my own middle-class upbringing was the powerful influence of peer and family interactions. Traditionally, Indian family structures offer rich social exposure, but the contemporary shift towards nuclear families often limits these interactions. Recognizing this, I ensured structured socialization through playdates, storytelling circles, and community gatherings, enabling my daughter to build diverse and meaningful relationships from an early age. This emphasis on social intelligence complemented her cognitive and emotional growth, preparing her for collaborative problem-solving and effective interpersonal relationships later in life.

I also learned firsthand the importance of teaching delayed gratification—an invaluable life skill extensively researched through studies like the Stanford Marshmallow Experiment. Encouraging my child to wait patiently for rewards, handle minor disappointments constructively, and persist through tasks without immediate gratification cultivated remarkable self-discipline and resilience in her. Such simple yet powerful training enabled her to develop mature decision-making skills and emotional stability, essential traits for lifelong success in a competitive, constantly evolving world.

Reflecting deeply, I now see clearly how critical early childhood is in the broader journey towards financial independence and career fulfillment. In Indian middle-class homes, a common mistake is assuming formal schooling alone guarantees future success. However, true empowerment comes from a holistic upbringing that balances cognitive stimulation, emotional maturity, self-reliance, and social skills. The foundational habits and mindsets developed in early childhood serve as stepping stones towards sustained financial discipline, career excellence, and overall life satisfaction.

Throughout this journey, the wisdom from prominent authors like Paul Tough (How Children Succeed) resonated deeply with my parenting approach, affirming my belief in cultivating resilience, curiosity, and character as equally significant, if not more, than academic grades alone. Such structured, intentional parenting provides children with enduring advantages—advantages I wish my parents had fully recognized and leveraged.

For middle-class Indian families today, it is essential to move beyond traditional academic-centric views. Understanding and embracing the transformative power of structured early childhood development—through interactive learning, emotional nurturing, independence-building, and social intelligence—is the key to equipping our children for a future not defined merely by survival or security, but thriving and fulfillment.

In essence, the first five years hold immense potential. They represent the formative blueprint for life's entire journey, echoing principles I learned as an architect: a strong, thoughtfully crafted foundation will always support lifelong growth, resilience, and success. By consciously investing in these foundational years, parents can shape confident, capable, and emotionally intelligent individuals, ready to navigate and excel in a complex and competitive world. This chapter embodies my deep belief and personal conviction that the most impactful journey to financial freedom and meaningful success begins, not in adulthood, but in the earliest days of a child's life.

Implementation of the Concept

Step A: Home-Schooling Basics, Early Learning Techniques, and Play-Based Education

Children learn best through play. Dr. John Medina, in *Brain Rules for Baby*, explains that play-based learning enhances creativity, strengthens problem-solving skills, and boosts memory retention. Instead of relying on rote memorization, Indian parents must embrace interactive learning methods that nurture curiosity. Some effective approaches include:

- **Storytelling:** Indian folklore, mythology, and moral stories help children develop a sense of right and wrong.
- **Sensory Play:** Activities such as playing with clay, water, or textured materials enhance cognitive and motor skills.
- **Music and Rhythm:** Exposure to music, nursery rhymes, and simple instruments can improve language

acquisition and concentration.

- **Basic Numeracy and Literacy:** Instead of pushing formal learning, parents can introduce numbers and letters through fun activities like counting household objects or identifying alphabets in books.

Step B: Developing Personal Responsibility, Self-Care Habits, and Basic Decision-Making Skills

By the age of three, children can begin taking small responsibilities, helping to build their confidence and self-reliance. In India, many middle-class households rely on domestic help for chores, but involving children in daily tasks fosters independence and discipline. Strategies for developing these skills include:

- **Self-Care Routines:** Teaching children to brush their teeth, dress themselves, and eat independently.
- **Household Contributions:** Involving children in sorting clothes, watering plants, or setting the table.
- **Decision-Making Opportunities:** Letting them choose between two outfits, decide on a bedtime story, or pick a meal option to develop autonomy.
- **Delayed Gratification Training:** Studies, such as the Stanford Marshmallow Experiment, show that children who learn to wait for rewards develop better self-control and long-term success habits.

Step C: Building Early Social Interactions, Emotional Intelligence, and Values-Driven

Upbringing

In Indian culture, family and community play a significant role in shaping a child's social skills. However, with nuclear families becoming the norm, parents must consciously create opportunities for social interaction. Emotional intelligence is equally critical. *The Whole-Brain Child* by Daniel Siegel emphasizes that children who learn to express emotions, manage conflicts, and understand empathy develop stronger relationships later in life. Parents can cultivate these skills through:

- **Structured Socialization:** Arranging playdates, engaging in storytelling circles, and exposing children to diverse social settings.
- **Modelling Positive Behaviour:** Children learn by observing their parents, so demonstrating patience, kindness, and active listening helps shape their emotional intelligence.
- **Encouraging Empathy:** Teaching children to share, help others, and recognize emotions in people around them.
- **Mindfulness Practices:** Simple breathing exercises or gratitude rituals can help children build self-awareness and emotional stability.

Social Proof & Learning from Experts

The principles discussed in this chapter are backed by research and insights from some of the most renowned experts in child development:

- **John Medina, *Brain Rules for Baby***: Highlights how play-based learning, emotional security, and social interactions enhance cognitive growth in young children.
- **Daniel J. Siegel & Tina Payne Bryson, *The Whole-Brain Child***: Offers insights into the neuroscience behind emotional regulation and how parents can help children integrate logic with emotions.
- **Paul Tough, *How Children Succeed***: Emphasizes the role of resilience, curiosity, and character in long-term success, rather than just academic achievement.

Final Thoughts

The first five years are **not just about preparing a child for school**—they are about preparing them for life. Indian middle-class families must look beyond academic excellence and invest in holistic development that nurtures curiosity, independence, and emotional intelligence. By **creating an enriching home environment,** actively engaging in a child's learning process, and leveraging the right tools and techniques, parents can lay a strong foundation for a child's future success. The journey to financial freedom and career fulfilment begins not at adulthood, but in childhood, and parents have the power to shape that trajectory from the very start.

Ages 5–12 | Building Core Values and Financial Literacy

The years between five and twelve serve as a bridge between early childhood and adolescence, marking a period of rapid cognitive, social, and emotional development. This is when children begin forming their core beliefs about money, relationships, discipline, and self-worth. Indian middle-class parents often focus entirely on academic performance during these years, prioritizing school grades over real-world skills. However, **this phase is when children need to be taught the fundamental values of financial literacy, emotional resilience, and independent thinking.** The habits developed now will shape their future ability to handle money, build relationships, and make decisions.

Who?

This chapter is for parents who are navigating the early school years of their children. Whether raising a child in a bustling Indian metro city or a small town, the principles of financial literacy, self-discipline, and emotional intelligence remain essential. Parents often struggle with balancing academic expectations with real-world education. This chapter helps them integrate financial wisdom, values, and practical decision-making into everyday learning.

Why?

Children at this age absorb values and lessons from their surroundings, parents, schools, and peers. Studies from the University of Cambridge suggest that financial habits begin forming as early as the age of seven. By the time children reach their teenage years, their attitude toward money and decision-making is already shaped. The gap between those who develop financial awareness and those who do not often results in drastic differences in life outcomes. Middle-class families, in particular, need to ensure that children grow up with financial wisdom rather than just academic excellence. Teaching them about active and passive income, the importance of savings, and responsible spending during these years prepares them for a stable and secure future.

What?

Education extends beyond classrooms and textbooks. True learning happens in daily interactions, experiences, and guided conversations. Parents must take an active role in helping children understand social values, community responsibility, and financial awareness. This means:

- Teaching them the difference between needs and wants, saving and spending, and risk and reward.

- Encouraging emotional intelligence—helping them process failures, setbacks, and peer interactions.
- Introducing real-world financial habits such as budgeting, earning money through small tasks, and long-term goal setting.
- Helping them develop problem-solving skills that will enable them to navigate future challenges independently.

Where?

Learning happens everywhere—at home, in school, within communities, and through cultural exposure. India's middle-class families have a unique advantage where education is considered a primary focus. However, parents must ensure that financial literacy and personal development are integrated into a child's everyday routine. Schools teach math, but they don't teach financial decision-making. Families instill values, but they often do not discuss the practical aspects of money management. A conscious effort is needed to bring both aspects together.

When?

This phase occurs between the ages of five and twelve, a critical time when children absorb knowledge like sponges. The habits they build now will either help or hinder their future financial stability and emotional well-being. These years must be used to:

- **Ages 5–7:** Introduce simple concepts like saving money in a piggy bank and differentiating between needs and wants.

- **Ages 7–9:** Engage children in small financial decisions, such as planning an outing within a budget or understanding the value of effort through small earnings (helping with simple home tasks for a reward).
- **Ages 9–12:** Teach them the basics of active and passive income, long-term goal setting, and emotional resilience in handling failure.

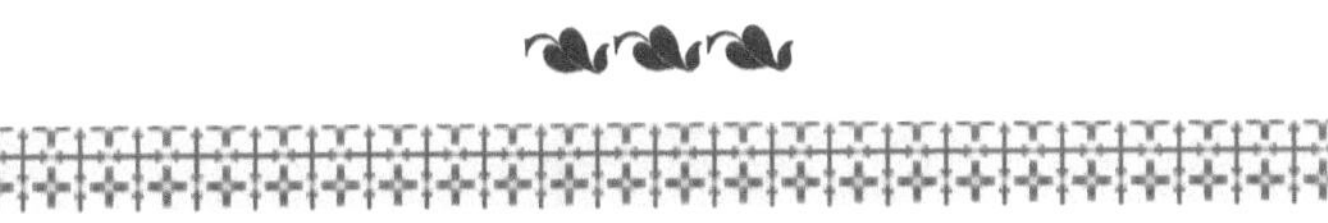

Perspective View

Between the ages of five and twelve, children embark on an extraordinary developmental journey, a bridge connecting their carefree early childhood and the complexities of adolescence. Reflecting on my own upbringing in a typical middle-class Indian household, I distinctly recall these years as pivotal. They weren't merely about school exams or strict discipline; they were about shaping the foundational attitudes that would later guide my relationships, financial decisions, and overall outlook on life. Like most Indian children of my generation, my parents prioritized academic performance above all else, believing top grades were synonymous with guaranteed success. It wasn't until later in life that I recognized the shortcomings of this traditional view. Grades alone could not shield me from real-world challenges, nor could they equip me with the crucial life skills necessary to navigate the complexities of adulthood—especially financial literacy and emotional intelligence.

My parents, diligent government employees, were products of a mindset where security and stability overshadowed risk-taking and innovation. Financial discussions at home were typically limited to saving for essentials or managing household budgets. Investments, passive income, or nuanced financial strategies were rarely, if ever, discussed. This gap in early financial education significantly shaped my initial approach to money—overly cautious, risk-averse, and predominantly reliant on active income from stable employment. It took years of unlearning and relearning to realize how critical these early formative years had been. Research from the University of Cambridge reinforces this insight, highlighting that children form lasting financial habits as early as seven years old. Middle-class families, particularly in India, unknowingly neglect a golden opportunity by deferring financial education until adolescence or adulthood.

Having traversed this challenging path myself, I now passionately advocate integrating financial literacy, emotional resilience, and independent thinking into children's everyday lives from these formative years. It's clear that education extends far beyond academics—it's about equipping children with the ability to discern between needs and wants, to distinguish active income (earned through effort) from passive income (earned from assets), and to grasp the importance of delayed gratification and disciplined savings. Simple practices like giving children an allowance and encouraging them to categorize spending into "save," "spend," and "share" jars instill financial responsibility and budgeting skills at an early age, something I wish my parents had done with me.

The cornerstone of building lasting wealth and security lies in understanding money's true nature and potential. Drawing inspiration from Robert Kiyosaki's Rich Dad Poor Dad for Teens, I realized that Indian parents must teach children not only the importance of saving but also the strategic value of investing. This can begin through practical, relatable methods: encouraging children to earn pocket money through small chores, explaining how investing time and effort yields rewards, and progressively introducing more complex concepts like passive income through interest or simple investments. Such tangible lessons help children appreciate money's true value beyond mere spending power.

Alongside financial literacy, fostering emotional resilience during these years is equally vital. Reflecting upon my childhood, failures—whether academic or personal—were often sources of deep anxiety rather than valuable lessons. My parents, like many in the middle-class Indian ethos, inadvertently shielded me from disappointments, focusing entirely on securing immediate comfort rather than building resilience. This protective stance, though well-intentioned, delayed my understanding of managing setbacks constructively. Stephen Covey's The 7 Habits of Highly Effective Families emphasizes that building resilience involves allowing children to experience minor setbacks and supporting them as they navigate these emotions independently. Practically, this could mean encouraging children to handle academic disappointments, failed attempts at creative endeavors, or social rejections with supportive guidance rather than immediate intervention.

Furthermore, independent thinking and decision-making skills were seldom consciously nurtured during my early years. Decisions, whether financial or personal, were typically made by my parents, leaving me little room for developing autonomy. Only in adulthood did I appreciate T. Harv Eker's assertion in The Secrets of the Millionaire Mind that a strong financial future depends significantly on mindset, early decision-making abilities, and personal confidence. Today, I encourage parents to involve their children in practical decisions, whether choosing between recreational activities within a set budget or deciding how best to allocate their savings. Activities that stimulate entrepreneurial thinking—such as small neighborhood businesses, craft sales, or participation in community fairs—teach children valuable lessons in responsibility, creative thinking, and financial independence.

Another crucial aspect often overlooked by traditional Indian parenting is managing peer influences. During my childhood, peer pressure subtly shaped my perspectives on material possessions, leading to unnecessary expenditures and impulsive decisions. Parents must address these influences proactively by guiding children to make confident, informed decisions independent of external validation. Discussing the difference between genuine needs and peer-driven wants fosters strong self-awareness and responsible spending habits that endure through adulthood.

Social responsibility and community engagement also greatly shape a child's character during this period. Although my family emphasized personal discipline and academic rigor, community participation and collective responsibility were rarely discussed. Encouraging children to partake in volunteering, charitable acts, or communal projects develops empathy, social awareness, and a broader worldview. Such experiences teach children that true fulfillment comes not merely from financial success but also from meaningful contributions to society.

Considering my experiences and recognizing gaps in traditional middle-class Indian parenting, I advocate a balanced, comprehensive approach. Academic excellence alone is insufficient for lifelong success. Parents must consciously integrate financial literacy, emotional resilience, independent thinking, and social responsibility into everyday life experiences during these formative years. Real-world financial training—budgeting, saving, investing, and understanding active versus passive income—should become part of routine interactions at home. Emotional maturity should be nurtured by letting children handle setbacks constructively. Independent thinking skills must be developed through active decision-making opportunities, entrepreneurial projects, and social interactions.

By proactively applying these strategies, parents can prepare their children to confidently face the future—not merely survive in it. The goal is raising individuals who are financially literate, emotionally resilient, and socially responsible, capable of navigating life's complexities without the fears and limitations common in the traditional middle-class narrative. Ultimately, success is about building character, financial wisdom, and emotional stability from a young age, creating a solid foundation for lifelong independence and prosperity.

Implementation of the Concept

Step A: Teaching Core Family Values, Emotional Resilience, and Community Engagement

A child's understanding of values is deeply influenced by their environment. Parents must ensure they create a culture of respect, kindness, and responsibility at home. **The 7 Habits of Highly Effective Families** by Stephen R. Covey emphasizes the importance of instilling lifelong values through family interactions.

- **Respect & Responsibility**: Assigning age-appropriate household responsibilities builds discipline. Children who contribute to family tasks develop a stronger work ethic and an understanding of responsibility.
- **Failure & Resilience**: Parents must teach that failure is part of growth. Encouraging children to handle small disappointments and setbacks early prepares them to manage stress and develop problem-solving abilities.
- **Community & Social Responsibility**: Encouraging children to participate in community activities such as donation drives, charity events, or volunteering helps instill a sense of contribution and awareness of the world beyond themselves.

Step B: Introducing Money Basics—Active vs. Passive Income, Savings, and Early Financial Habits

Financial literacy must start early, not as an academic subject but as a life skill. **Rich Dad Poor Dad for Teens** by Robert Kiyosaki simplifies financial concepts for young minds, making it easier for parents to introduce these ideas in daily life.

- **Savings & Budgeting:** Start by giving children a small allowance and teaching them to allocate portions for spending, saving, and giving. Use clear jars labeled "Spend," "Save," and "Share" to make money management tangible.
- **Active vs. Passive Income:** Explain that active income is earned through work (chores, tasks), while passive income grows over time (interest, investments). A simple example is letting them "invest" money in a parent's business (helping with simple work) and receiving small returns.
- **Delayed Gratification:** Studies show that children who learn to delay gratification are more likely to succeed in life (Stanford Marshmallow Experiment). Encouraging kids to wait before making purchases builds financial discipline.

Step C: Encouraging Independent Thinking and Decision-Making Skills

The ability to think independently and make decisions is a crucial life skill. **The Secrets of the Millionaire Mind** by T. Harv Eker highlights that mindset plays a significant role in financial success. Parents must help children develop critical thinking abilities from an early age.

- **Making Choices:** Involve children in financial decisions, such as comparing product prices, deciding between different entertainment options, or choosing between immediate and future rewards.

- **Entrepreneurial Thinking:** Encourage small business ideas, such as setting up a lemonade stand, selling handmade crafts, or organizing a garage sale. This builds confidence, creativity, and a sense of ownership over money.
- **Problem-Solving:** Teach children to evaluate risks and rewards by playing strategy games, encouraging debates, or allowing them to make mistakes and learn from them.

Social Proof & Learning from Experts

The principles in this chapter are backed by insights from financial and behavioral experts:

- **Robert Kiyosaki, *Rich Dad Poor Dad for Teens*:** Teaches young minds the basics of financial independence, savings, and smart money habits.
- **Stephen R. Covey, *The 7 Habits of Highly Effective Families*:** Emphasizes the importance of values, emotional discipline, and character-building in early life.
- **T. Harv Eker, *The Secrets of the Millionaire Mind*:** Focuses on how financial success is built on mindset, early habits, and decision-making skills.

Final Thoughts

The years between five and twelve must be used to **build financial awareness, emotional resilience, and independent thinking** in children. Indian middle-class families should **go beyond traditional academic success** and ensure their children **understand the value of money, the importance of financial planning, and the impact of responsible decision-making.** The goal is to raise **confident, financially aware individuals** who can navigate adulthood without struggling with financial illiteracy. By integrating financial lessons into daily life, parents can prepare their children not just for school, but for life itself.

CHAPTER THREE

Ages 12–19 | Cultivating a Wealth Mindset and Escaping Middle-Class Traps

The teenage years, spanning from 12 to 19, are a defining period in a person's life. This phase determines not only academic direction but also financial habits, career aspirations, social influences, and personal values. Teenagers start forming their identity and begin making independent decisions. However, without the right guidance, they can fall into unhealthy financial and personal habits that could affect them for years to come. **Middle-class Indian families often focus exclusively on academic performance, assuming that financial literacy, relationship management, and career readiness will develop later.** This is a critical mistake. The teenage years are when financial behaviours are hardwired, relationships begin shaping future life choices, and career directions start taking form.

Who?

This chapter is meant for teenagers and their parents who want to ensure financial awareness, self-development, and emotional intelligence during the crucial teenage years. Indian middle-class parents, while deeply invested in their children's education, often overlook financial preparedness and personal growth beyond academics. The goal here is to bridge that gap by focusing on real-world skills, investment basics, peer influence, and relationships.

Why?

Teenagers are bombarded with external influences from social media, peers, advertising, and societal expectations. Studies from Cambridge University indicate that financial behaviors are largely set by age 14, meaning that waiting until adulthood to discuss money management is already too late. Additionally, teenagers begin forming serious relationships during this time, and their understanding of emotional intelligence, self-worth, and decision-making will impact their future family life and career. Middle-class Indian families must proactively equip their teenagers with financial literacy, social intelligence, and career-building skills to ensure a successful and stress-free future.

What?

This phase is about refining the lessons learned in childhood and applying them to real-world situations. Parents must help their teenagers understand:

- The importance of choosing the right friends and social circle, as **"you are the average of the five people you spend the most time with"** (Jim Rohn).
- How money works, including investment basics, insurance, and the importance of saving.
- Emotional intelligence, how to navigate peer pressure, and the foundations of long-term relationships.
- The concept of career-building—not just academic achievement, but skill acquisition, networking, and personal branding.
- The significance of developing a wealth mindset rather than merely earning a salary in adulthood.

Where?

Teenagers develop financial habits and social behaviours both at home and in school. However, Indian school curriculums rarely touch upon personal finance, investing, or wealth-building. Learning must take place outside the classroom—through conversations at home, exposure to financial discussions, practical applications (such as managing small amounts of money), and mentorship from financially literate individuals. Parents must foster an environment where financial education and emotional intelligence are as important as academic achievements.

When?

Teenagers begin to make significant life decisions between the ages of 12 and 19, making this the perfect time to guide them towards financial and social independence.

- **Ages 12–14:** Understanding peer influence, money basics, and decision-making skills.
- **Ages 15–17:** Learning investment concepts, budgeting skills, emotional resilience, and the power of networking.
- **Ages 18–19:** Applying financial knowledge through actual investments, securing insurance, understanding career paths, and planning long-term financial goals.

Perspective View

The teenage years, between ages twelve and nineteen, represent one of life's most defining periods. As someone who grew up in a middle-class working Indian family, I can vividly recall how this crucial stage shaped my financial understanding, personal values, and future ambitions. It was a phase of immense curiosity and vulnerability, heavily influenced by peers, media, and societal expectations. My parents, like most Indian middle-class families, prioritized academic performance above all else, assuming that financial wisdom, relationship skills, and career strategies would naturally develop over time. Unfortunately, that assumption overlooks how deeply foundational teenage experiences truly are. Cambridge University research highlights a striking reality: most lifelong financial habits are established by age fourteen. Reflecting on my own adolescence, I now realize how vital proactive education in financial literacy, relationship management, and career planning is during these formative years.

Growing up, my understanding of money was basic—limited to pocket money, modest savings, and the vague knowledge that financial security came from holding a stable job. Discussions about investments, passive income, or financial planning rarely, if ever, took place at home. My peers, too, were largely uneducated in managing money. Social interactions were frequently centered around status symbols and materialistic comparisons, a narrative amplified by advertisements and social media. As Jim Rohn famously stated, "You are the average of the five people you spend the most time with." Unfortunately, without guidance, many teenagers gravitate towards peers who prioritize instant gratification and superficial values over ambition, financial discipline, and self-improvement.

Indian middle-class families, in their pursuit of academic excellence, unintentionally neglect essential aspects of real-world preparedness. The prevailing mindset often delays financial education and emotional intelligence, mistakenly believing these skills will develop naturally later. Yet this very delay is why so many young adults today face overwhelming confusion and stress when confronted with financial decisions, career crossroads, or relationship challenges. Financial literacy is not an innate trait but a carefully cultivated skill. My experience taught me the importance of teaching teenagers early on about budgeting, saving, investing, and responsibly managing money. Even modest exposure to these concepts can significantly impact a teenager's financial confidence and capability.

Implementing financial education practically means introducing teenagers to simple budgeting exercises, helping them understand the value of delayed gratification, and explaining foundational concepts such as active versus passive income, compounding interest, and prudent investment options like mutual funds and fixed deposits. Books like Morgan Housel's The Psychology of Money emphasize how financial success hinges more on disciplined behavior than financial knowledge alone. This insight aligns perfectly with teenage learning—small yet consistent financial habits formed early can lead to substantial financial stability later in life.

Moreover, I deeply understand the power and pitfalls of peer influence during teenage years. In my adolescence, the desire to fit in often led to impulsive spending and superficial priorities, undermining my ability to save or invest. Today, teenagers face even stronger peer pressures, compounded by constant exposure to curated lives on Instagram and YouTube. Helping teens discern between genuine needs and socially-driven wants is critical. Discussions at home about peer pressure, materialism, and digital validation should be commonplace. Encouraging teenagers to carefully choose their social circles, participate in extracurricular activities, and foster meaningful friendships can nurture ambition, discipline, and emotional stability. Research from the National Bureau of Economic Research confirms peer influence profoundly impacts decision-making and future aspirations, further emphasizing the necessity of consciously managing social interactions.

Equally significant is relationship education. Reflecting back, my teenage years were filled with emotional upheavals and misunderstandings, many of which stemmed from inadequate knowledge about emotional intelligence and healthy relationships. In Indian culture, openly discussing relationship dynamics or emotional health is often neglected or delayed until adulthood, causing teenagers to navigate complex emotions without adequate support. Books like John Gray's Men Are from Mars, Women Are from Venus provide valuable insights, helping teenagers understand fundamental differences in emotional processing, communication, and expectations within relationships. Encouraging open dialogue about relationship values, long-term compatibility, and emotional resilience can profoundly influence a teenager's capacity to handle relationships constructively, thus avoiding meaningless short-term infatuations and distractions.

Emotional intelligence—understanding, expressing, and managing one's emotions—is another critical life skill often overlooked during adolescence. The teenage years are a testing ground for emotional stability, with academic pressures, peer rejections, relationship setbacks, and personal failures being commonplace. My teenage self struggled significantly to cope with setbacks because failure was often viewed negatively rather than as a natural learning opportunity. Parents must actively foster emotional resilience, helping teenagers understand that failures and rejections are integral to growth. Cal Newport's So Good They Can't Ignore You highlights how sustained career success derives not merely from passion but from disciplined skills and emotional stability cultivated through overcoming setbacks.

Lastly, career planning must move beyond traditional academics and involve real-world skills, networking, and personal branding early on. My journey into architecture, a profession that uniquely blends creativity, precision, and project management, taught me that career success often depends on transferable skills, disciplined learning, and strategic networking rather than mere academic qualifications. Encouraging teenagers to explore diverse fields, identify high-income skills, and build professional connections through internships, extracurricular activities, or mentorship programs can significantly enhance their career preparedness and adaptability.

My journey—transitioning from a traditionally constrained mindset to one of financial independence, emotional intelligence, and strategic career planning—highlights the transformative potential of proactive teenage education. By addressing financial literacy, peer influence, emotional resilience, relationship skills, and career preparedness during these critical years, parents can equip their children with comprehensive life skills that far exceed mere academic success. The teenage years are not simply about grades or diplomas; they represent the cornerstone of adulthood, where the foundations of financial security, emotional stability, career fulfillment, and meaningful relationships are laid.

Middle-class Indian families must consciously prioritize these aspects. Real-life lessons integrated into daily interactions, open dialogues at home about money, friendships, emotional health, and relationships, and practical experiences such as budgeting, investing, and networking can prepare teenagers for the realities of adulthood. Such comprehensive education not only prevents unhealthy financial or emotional habits from forming but also instills confidence, independence, and maturity. My personal journey, with all its challenges and lessons, underscores the immense value of early, deliberate guidance. By understanding and embracing these lessons, families can ensure their teenagers not only survive but thrive, achieving lifelong financial freedom, emotional resilience, fulfilling relationships, and sustained career success.

Implementation of the Concept

Step A: Understanding Peer Influence, Friendships, and the Importance of Choosing the Right Environment

Teenagers are heavily influenced by their peers. Their habits, confidence, and ambitions are shaped by the people they spend time with. Research by the National Bureau of Economic Research shows that peer influence plays a significant role in financial behaviour, career aspirations, and decision-making skills.

- **Choosing the Right Friends:** Encourage teenagers to evaluate their social circle. Are they surrounded by ambitious, disciplined individuals, or do they spend time with people who encourage reckless behaviour?
- **Avoiding Negative Peer Pressure:** Teach them that financial responsibility means resisting impulsive purchases, unnecessary social status spending, and materialistic comparison.
- **Understanding Social Media Influence:** Teenagers today are more influenced by Instagram, YouTube, and influencers than ever before. Parents must discuss **"social media vs. reality"** and help their children build confidence without seeking validation through material possessions.
- **Networking and Personal Branding:** The teenage years are the best time to start building strong connections.

Encourage networking through extracurricular activities, online courses, and mentorship programs.

Step B: Learning Investment Basics, Insurance, and Money Management

Financial literacy must begin before adulthood. **The Psychology of Money** by Morgan Housel highlights that money management is more about behaviour than knowledge. Parents must help their teenagers develop responsible money habits early.

- **Savings and Budgeting:** Introduce teenagers to tracking their spending and setting financial goals. Even a small personal budget teaches discipline.
- **Understanding Investments:** Concepts like SIPs, compounding interest, and passive income must be introduced gradually. Allow teenagers to start investing small amounts in fixed deposits or mutual funds with parental guidance.
- **Basics of Insurance:** Many young adults make poor insurance choices simply because they were never taught its importance. Teenagers should learn about health, term, and vehicle insurance as part of their financial education.
- **Avoiding Debt Traps:** Teaching teenagers about the risks of credit cards, loans, and impulsive spending can save them from years of financial hardship later in life.

Step C: Developing Emotional Intelligence and Forming Healthy Relationships

Emotional intelligence plays a crucial role in financial decisions, personal happiness, and professional success. **So Good They Can't Ignore You** by Cal Newport emphasizes that career success is built on skill and discipline rather than just passion. Similarly, strong relationships require effort, self-awareness, and emotional stability.

- **Understanding Relationship Dynamics:** Teach teenagers the **difference between short-term attraction and long-term compatibility** in friendships and romantic relationships.
- **Handling Rejections & Failures:** Many young people struggle with rejections in friendships, academics, or early relationships. Parents should normalize setbacks as learning opportunities rather than personal failures.
- **Managing Emotions & Self-Worth:** Building self-confidence reduces the need for external validation. Encourage activities that promote personal growth, such as fitness, hobbies, and skill-building.

Social Proof & Learning from Experts

The concepts discussed in this chapter are based on insights from experts in finance, psychology, and career development:

- **Morgan Housel, *The Psychology of Money***: Teaches the behavioural aspects of money and how early financial habits shape adulthood.
- **Jonathan Self, *The Teenage Guide to Money***: A simplified approach to financial literacy for young minds.
- **Cal Newport, *So Good They Can't Ignore You***: Emphasizes why skill-building and disciplined learning matter more than just academic qualifications.

Final Thoughts

The teenage years are **not just about academic success**—they are about preparing for life. Middle-class Indian families must go beyond **traditional education and ensure teenagers learn essential financial, social, and emotional skills.** By integrating money management, peer influence awareness, and emotional intelligence into their daily lives, parents can raise **confident, financially literate young adults who are ready to face the world.**

The foundation for financial freedom, career success, and fulfilling relationships starts in **teenage years**—not in adulthood.

CHAPTER FOUR

Ages 19–26 | Mastering Career, Finances, and Relationships

The years between 19 and 26 represent a transformative period of growth and pivotal decisions. Young adults transition from academic environments to professional realms, from dependence to independence, from learners to earners. The decisions taken during this period set foundational stones for future financial prosperity, career trajectory, and personal fulfilment. **For most middle-class Indian youth, this transition is fraught with confusion, compounded by limited guidance beyond academic pursuits. Schools and families often overlook critical skills like financial literacy, relationship intelligence, and strategic career planning.** However, success in the real world demands proficiency in these very domains.

Who?

This chapter is intended for ambitious young Indian professionals, college students, and fresh graduates determined to secure financial stability, career success, and meaningful personal relationships. Indian middle-class culture typically prioritizes academic achievements, but modern success extends beyond the traditional employment paths of medicine, engineering, or government services. Today's competitive environment demands diversification and innovation.

Why?

Choices made during the ages of 19 to 26 dramatically influence lifelong financial independence, professional success, and personal happiness. According to the National Bureau of Economic Research, those who begin investing early accrue significantly greater wealth due to the power of compounding. Additionally, emotional intelligence research emphasizes that those who master interpersonal skills build stronger personal relationships and professional networks, enhancing their long-term satisfaction and success.

What?

This stage is about deliberate career-building, wealth accumulation strategies, and careful relationship choices. To navigate these successfully, individuals should:

- Develop one high-income primary skill, such as Architecture, Medicine, Law, or Chartered Accountancy, complemented by secondary monetizable hobbies or skills.
- Master financial literacy early, encompassing saving, investing, financial planning, and security.

- Cultivate emotional intelligence, relationship selection criteria, and learn from relationship fundamentals like those outlined in John Gray's "Men Are from Mars, Women Are from Venus."
- Build a proactive growth mindset, constantly upgrading skills, adapting to evolving opportunities, and avoiding distractions such as meaningless short-term infatuations or peer pressure.

Where?

Professional skills are cultivated through internships, entry-level positions, self-directed learning platforms, mentorship, and real-world practice. Financial education is gathered from expert literature, trusted mentors, and practical application, while relationship intelligence comes through personal experiences, reflective learning, and structured personal development.

When?

The 19–26 age range consists of three strategic phases:

- **Ages 19–21:** Exploration and experimentation with skills, personal interests, and potential career paths.
- **Ages 22–24:** Early career growth, establishing disciplined financial practices, stabilizing primary income, and refining professional identity.
- **Ages 25–26:** Consolidation phase—actively investing, creating multiple income streams, building strong, meaningful relationships, and planning long-term goals.

Perspective View

The period between ages nineteen and twenty-six marks perhaps the most transformative years of anyone's life—a phase that I vividly recall from my own experience growing up in a middle-class working Indian family. These were the years when academic pursuits transitioned into professional realities, when theoretical learning had to confront practical application. Raised within the typical middle-class Indian mindset, my family emphasized academic excellence above everything else, believing firmly that securing a good degree and landing a stable job would ensure lifelong comfort. However, as I stepped out into the real world, I quickly discovered that this conventional approach, while important, was incomplete. It didn't account for critical skills such as financial literacy, relationship intelligence, or strategic career planning—all of which became glaringly important as I navigated early adulthood.

Like many of my peers, I grew up with limited exposure to financial education. Conversations about wealth creation, passive income, or financial planning were virtually non-existent at home. Instead, financial advice was typically reduced to the simple mantra: earn money and save carefully. Only upon entering the professional world did I realize that merely earning and saving were insufficient strategies to build true financial security.

Studies by the National Bureau of Economic Research highlight the immense advantage early investors hold due to compounding interest, a concept I learned only through experience. If I had been educated earlier about investment fundamentals such as mutual funds, equities, and systematic investment plans, my financial trajectory would have been vastly improved. Today, I strongly advocate for young adults to start mastering wealth-building strategies early, including disciplined budgeting, understanding insurance and security planning, and avoiding lifestyle inflation. Books like Tim Ferriss's The 4-Hour Workweek offer invaluable strategies, emphasizing a structured, automated approach to financial management—something I wish had been a part of my education during my own early twenties.

Alongside financial skills, the importance of developing a high-income primary skill became apparent early in my professional journey. In India, certain professions like architecture, medicine, law, and chartered accountancy offer significant stability and income potential, largely due to their legally recognized professional status. My personal choice to pursue architecture significantly shaped my understanding of career success. Architecture not only provided financial stability but also nurtured an entrepreneurial mindset—forcing me to think creatively, strategically, and systematically. India's rapid urban growth and infrastructure expansion make architecture uniquely rewarding, a profession that blends technical precision with innovative vision. However, relying solely on a primary skill, even one as lucrative as architecture, felt inadequate in a dynamic economic environment. Hence, I actively cultivated monetizable hobbies and secondary skills such as content writing, digital marketing, and online consulting.

MJ DeMarco's The Millionaire Fastlane emphasizes this exact principle, advocating for diverse income streams to ensure financial resilience. Young Indian professionals today must proactively cultivate multiple revenue channels—through freelancing, blogging, content creation, or investment dividends—to fortify their financial independence against market volatility.

One of the most underestimated yet crucial aspects of adulthood I discovered was relationship intelligence and partner selection. The quality of personal relationships profoundly affects career trajectory, emotional health, and overall life satisfaction—something I observed clearly within my own journey. In Indian society, relationship conversations are often either trivialized or overly romanticized, rarely treated with practical seriousness. However, choosing a supportive, emotionally intelligent partner who shares your vision can profoundly enhance your life's journey. Books like John Gray's Men Are from Mars, Women Are from Venus opened my eyes to the importance of understanding fundamental differences in communication, emotional processing, and expectations within relationships. Had I known this earlier, many misunderstandings and emotional challenges during my young adulthood would have been easier to navigate.

I also learned the hard way about the pitfalls of short-term distractions—temporary infatuations or peer pressures that often divert focus from long-term objectives. My early twenties were full of such distractions, fueled by social comparisons and the incessant need to belong. Only later did I realize how much valuable time was lost, time that could have been invested in skill-building, financial planning, or meaningful relationship formation. Cultivating emotional intelligence and maintaining clarity about long-term goals became essential. Balancing personal relationships and professional ambitions requires deliberate choice and thoughtful action—prioritizing partners and friendships that offer mutual growth, support, and alignment in values.

The age range between nineteen and twenty-six is ideally structured into three strategic phases, a concept I grasped only in hindsight. Initially (ages 19–21), it is beneficial to explore various skills and interests, clarifying personal ambitions. Subsequently (ages 22–24), a disciplined, focused approach towards financial literacy, career specialization, and early investment must be established. Finally (ages 25–26), consolidating these foundations through strategic investments, multiple income streams, and meaningful relationships lays the groundwork for lifelong prosperity and satisfaction. During these phases, proactive learning, structured goal setting, and consistent discipline are paramount.

The personal growth I experienced during these critical years was shaped not merely by academic achievement or professional advancement but significantly by financial wisdom, relationship intelligence, and an entrepreneurial mindset. Meg Jay, in her influential book The Defining Decade, articulates precisely why decisions made in one's twenties have outsized influence on future success and satisfaction. Reflecting on my experiences, I fully concur. The choices regarding investments, career skills, and personal relationships made during these years profoundly influence long-term trajectories.

The traditional middle-class Indian narrative, which emphasizes stability through conventional academic paths and jobs, requires updating. Modern success demands more than academic degrees; it requires diversified skills, proactive financial strategies, and intelligent relationship choices. By consciously addressing these aspects, young Indian professionals can break away from restrictive middle-class paradigms, creating independent, prosperous, and fulfilling lives.

Ultimately, the years from nineteen to twenty-six represent not merely a transition from academics to the workplace but a profound transformation into mature adulthood. Success during this phase demands financial literacy, high-income skill cultivation, emotional intelligence, relationship management, and disciplined planning. My journey from traditional middle-class limitations to genuine independence underscores the necessity of these skills. Today, I advocate strongly for this comprehensive approach—one I wish I had encountered sooner. The foundations laid during these years do not merely support financial stability; they foster lifelong satisfaction, meaningful relationships, and true prosperity.

Implementation of the Concept

Step A: Cultivating High-Income Skills and Monetizable Hobbies

In a volatile economy, job security is not guaranteed, as highlighted by MJ DeMarco in "The Millionaire Fastlane." Young professionals should proactively build diversified income streams:

- **Primary Skill Development:** Architecture, as one of the few professions in India legally recognized with monetizable signatures, presents exceptional income and career stability opportunities. India's rapid urbanization and infrastructure growth present architects with substantial earning potential.
- **Diversifying Skills:** Skills in digital marketing, finance, data science, and content creation offer significant earning potential and complement traditional professions.
- **Passive and Secondary Income:** Create additional revenue through blogging, freelancing, YouTube, stock investing, affiliate marketing, or rental income, leveraging multiple revenue streams to ensure financial resilience.
- **Entrepreneurial Mindset:** View careers not as static jobs but dynamic opportunities, consistently building assets like digital products, intellectual property, or rental properties.

Step B: Mastering Wealth-Building Strategies

Many Indian families teach income generation without teaching money management. Books like "The 4-Hour Workweek" by Tim Ferriss emphasize systematic financial strategies:

- **Budgeting and Financial Discipline:** Use the 50-30-20 budgeting rule (50% essentials, 30% lifestyle, 20% savings/investments) and automate savings to ensure consistent growth.

- **Early Investments:** Understand mutual funds, equities, real estate investments, and the power of compound interest to build significant long-term wealth.
- **Insurance and Security Planning:** Prioritize health, term, and asset insurance alongside building emergency funds to manage unforeseen financial setbacks effectively.
- **Avoiding Lifestyle Inflation:** Maintain a comfortable yet modest lifestyle, strategically managing income increases to enhance wealth accumulation rather than lifestyle expenses.

Step C: Relationship Fundamentals and Partner Selection

Relationships significantly impact career success and personal fulfilment. Harvard's Grant Study underscores the profound impact quality relationships have on overall happiness:

- **Choosing the Right Life Partner:** Evaluate potential life partners on compatibility, shared values, career support, emotional intelligence, and long-term alignment rather than transient attraction.
- **Understanding Emotional Dynamics:** Utilize insights from John Gray's "Men Are from Mars, Women Are from Venus," recognizing fundamental emotional differences and communication styles between genders.
- **Avoiding Short-term Distractions:** Minimize time invested in meaningless, short-term infatuations or peer pressure-driven relationships, which can distract from long-term goals.

- **Balancing Career and Relationships:** Select partners who complement career ambitions, ensuring mutual support and stability rather than becoming liabilities.

Social Proof & Expert Insights

- **"Men Are from Mars, Women Are from Venus" by John Gray:** Essential for understanding gender dynamics and enhancing relationship management, critical for long-term life planning.
- **"The Millionaire Fastlane" by MJ DeMarco:** A guide on accelerated wealth creation beyond traditional job dependency.
- **"The Defining Decade" by Meg Jay:** Highlights the critical importance of decisions made in the 20s, encouraging strategic action during this pivotal life stage.

Final Thoughts

The years between 19 and 26 are the most strategic for laying the foundation of financial independence, professional excellence, and fulfilling relationships.

Middle-class Indian professionals must consciously break away from conventional approaches, embracing modern financial literacy, diversified skill-building, and informed relationship choices.

Young professionals who proactively manage their financial literacy, career growth, and relationships in this decade set themselves up for lasting success, wealth, and happiness. **By mastering these critical life areas, you'll transition from mere survival to meaningful success—securing financial independence and creating a rewarding, prosperous life.**

Ages 26–33 | Maximizing Earnings, Accelerating Wealth Creation, and Building Family Foundations

The late 20s and early 30s represent a transformative era in the lives of young Indian professionals, marking peak earning potential, significant career advancements, and crucial personal decisions such as marriage and parenthood. For many in the Indian middle class, this period can either lead to substantial long-term wealth creation or result in stagnation due to lifestyle inflation and lack of strategic financial planning. It is during these pivotal years that one should **strategically maximize their earnings, diversify investments, and, crucially, settle down with the right long-term partner** to lay a stable foundation for family life and future prosperity.

Who?

Young professionals, entrepreneurs, and freelancers aged between 26 and 33, especially those in licensed professions such as architecture, medicine, law, finance, or senior corporate roles, stand at the threshold of substantial income growth and wealth accumulation opportunities. These individuals are uniquely positioned to leverage their skills, networks, and resources to significantly scale their wealth.

Why?

According to the Economic Policy Institute, salaries typically witness their steepest growth between the ages of 27 and 35, offering the optimal window for strategic financial decisions. Concurrently, life-changing responsibilities such as marriage, parenthood, and homeownership emerge, necessitating a keen balance between career aspirations, financial planning, and relationship choices. Harvard Business Review studies reinforce that professionals who settle with supportive life partners during this phase achieve not only higher career satisfaction but also greater wealth accumulation and personal fulfillment. Establishing a stable family foundation at this age allows your children to grow into contributors rather than remain dependents in your prime earning years.

What?

This phase demands a multifaceted strategy that includes:

- **Maximizing Primary Income:** Leveraging professional growth to significantly enhance earning potential.
- **Strategic Investment Planning:** Developing a diversified investment portfolio to ensure long-term financial security.
- **Multiple Income Streams:** Creating sustainable side incomes to buffer against economic uncertainties.
- **Settling Down:** Selecting a supportive long-term partner, strategically timing marriage, and starting a family.
- **Optimal Family Planning:** Having children at an age when you have both emotional maturity and financial readiness, thus ensuring your family supports rather than strains your financial goals.

Where?

Success in this phase involves strategic efforts across multiple platforms:

- Corporate and entrepreneurial environments for maximizing earnings.
- Financial markets, real estate investments, and personal ventures to build wealth.
- Family and personal life for cultivating supportive relationships and raising a family.

When?

- **Ages 26–28:** Accelerate career progression, expand earning capabilities, and actively seek a compatible life partner.
- **Ages 28–30:** Settle into marriage, begin establishing multiple income streams, and initiate family planning.
- **Ages 30–33:** Optimize and diversify investment portfolios, establish passive incomes, and focus on family security and having children.

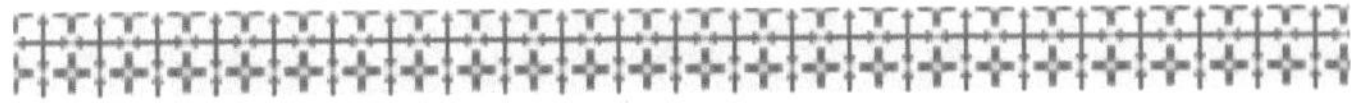

Perspective View

Growing up in a typical Indian middle-class family, the late twenties and early thirties were often portrayed as the pinnacle of life—a period marked by significant career growth, financial gains, and crucial decisions about marriage and family. Like many of my peers, I entered this phase filled with both ambition and anxiety, recognizing its importance but unsure exactly how to maximize my potential. In our community, conversations around these critical years tended to focus narrowly on traditional milestones: earning a stable income, getting married, purchasing a home, and eventually starting a family. But there was little discussion about strategic wealth creation, the power of diversified investments, or the importance of consciously selecting the right life partner who would actively support one's long-term vision. As I navigated through this defining period of my life, I began to understand that real success required far more intentionality than simply following traditional scripts.

During this phase, professionals in fields such as architecture, medicine, law, finance, and senior corporate roles typically reach their peak earning years. This fact, supported by studies from institutions like the Economic Policy Institute, reveals the critical importance of maximizing one's income potential between ages 27 and 35. Yet, merely earning more doesn't guarantee financial security. In my journey, I quickly realized the pitfalls of lifestyle inflation, a trap all too common within the Indian middle class. Watching friends and family upgrading lifestyles with each salary increment, I noticed that higher income often translated directly into higher expenditures, limiting genuine wealth accumulation. Recognizing this trend, I consciously chose instead to reinvest a substantial portion of my increased income into diversified assets, leveraging my professional growth not for immediate gratification but for long-term financial independence.

As I progressed in my career as an architect, a licensed professional uniquely positioned in the Indian economy, I experienced firsthand the immense potential for wealth creation. Architecture is one of India's few recognized professions where a signature has monetary value, underscoring the earning and entrepreneurial potential this career offers. I quickly learned, however, that professional growth alone was insufficient. Inspired by Naval Ravikant's insights from "The Almanack of Naval Ravikant," I actively pursued diversification, investing strategically in equity markets, real estate, and fixed-income instruments. The concept of passive income was transformative for me; guided by Robert Kiyosaki's teachings in "Rich Dad's Cashflow Quadrant," I began shifting from purely active income generation towards investments capable of producing long-term returns with minimal ongoing effort. Real estate investments in particular offered rental income streams, providing financial stability beyond my active work hours.

The idea of multiple income streams further enriched my financial journey. During this time, influenced by Robert G. Allen's "Multiple Streams of Income," I pursued side businesses, freelance consulting, and content creation. Initially challenging, these secondary streams eventually turned into reliable sources of income, reducing dependence on my primary profession. This diversification not only offered greater financial security but significantly increased my resilience against economic uncertainties. By maintaining a portfolio that combined equity investments, real estate rentals, dividend-paying stocks, and entrepreneurial ventures, I effectively insulated my financial health from market volatility.

However, achieving financial independence is not solely about money. Perhaps the most critical decision during these transformative years is choosing the right life partner. Drawing upon wisdom from Thomas Stanley's "The Millionaire Next Door," I understood that stable, supportive relationships are vital for sustainable wealth accumulation and overall life satisfaction. Observing my own family and peers, it became clear that personal fulfillment and career success were profoundly influenced by relationship quality. My decision to marry was guided by compatibility, shared values, mutual support, and alignment with long-term goals rather than fleeting attraction or external pressures. Building upon insights from John Gray's "Men Are from Mars, Women Are from Venus," my wife and I focused on open communication, emotional intelligence, and joint financial planning, significantly strengthening our personal and financial foundation.

Strategically timing parenthood also became a crucial part of my personal roadmap. Research consistently indicates that starting a family in one's late twenties or early thirties combines emotional maturity and financial readiness, a balance critical to creating a stable home environment. Within Indian culture, children are often viewed as both a source of joy and significant financial responsibility. I realized that by having children at an optimal age—when earnings were robust and investments diversified—my family would not become a burden but rather grow alongside my career trajectory. Careful budgeting for child-related expenses, education, healthcare, and lifestyle choices ensured that my family life supported rather than strained our overall financial goals.

Moreover, establishing financial discipline early allowed my children to grow up learning vital financial lessons by observation, gradually becoming active contributors to the family's overall prosperity rather than mere dependents. The idea of generational wealth-building became central to our financial decisions, reflecting a significant departure from traditional middle-class short-term thinking. By consciously avoiding extravagant lifestyle inflation and focusing instead on stable, disciplined financial practices, we cultivated an environment where wealth became sustainable, deeply embedded into our family culture.

Ultimately, the transformative years between 26 and 33 offer unparalleled opportunities for young Indian professionals to achieve meaningful prosperity and deep personal fulfillment—but only if navigated strategically. For me, these crucial years required deliberate choices across multiple domains: aggressively maximizing professional earnings, carefully building diversified investment portfolios, consciously developing multiple income streams, thoughtfully choosing a life partner, and strategically timing family expansion. Rather than passively drifting through life's traditional milestones, success demanded proactive, intentional decision-making in every area.

Reflecting upon my journey, it is evident that escaping the classic Indian middle-class trap of working solely for immediate comfort demands purposeful action and a clear long-term vision. Young professionals must resist societal pressures of superficial lifestyle upgrades and short-term gratification, instead committing to structured financial growth, emotional maturity, and relationship stability. Strategic financial planning, thoughtful family formation, and careful management of personal relationships serve as the foundations of lasting success, transforming peak earning years into a launching pad for lifelong prosperity.

Today, as I look back, these decisive years stand out as pivotal—marked by intense growth, critical learning, and foundational decisions. While challenging, this period presented unique opportunities to shape my future, escaping financial dependency and fostering genuine independence. I am convinced that every young Indian professional, armed with this understanding and strategic approach, can similarly leverage these critical years to build enduring wealth, profound personal happiness, and a legacy of true success.

Implementation of the Concept

Step A: Maximizing Primary Earnings

Enhancing primary income is foundational to wealth accumulation. As Naval Ravikant outlines in *"The Almanack of Naval Ravikant,"* financial independence is best achieved through leveraging one's skills for maximum earnings potential.

- **Corporate Professionals:** Pursue leadership roles and strategic promotions actively.
- **Entrepreneurs:** Expand operations, reinvest profits intelligently, and build strong brand equity.
- **Freelancers & Consultants:** Diversify services, adjust pricing strategies, and secure long-term client relationships.
- **Licensed Professionals (Architects, Doctors, Lawyers, CAs):** Enhance expertise, network extensively, acquire high-value clients, and command premium rates due to the specialized nature of their professions.

Step B: Building a Diversified Investment Portfolio

Robert Kiyosaki, in *"Rich Dad's Cashflow Quadrant,"* emphasizes transitioning from active to passive income to build sustainable wealth.

- **Equity Investments:** Invest strategically in index funds, blue-chip stocks, and ETFs to harness long-term compounding.

- **Real Estate:** Build rental income streams and consider investments in REITs.
- **Fixed Income Instruments:** Utilize secure options such as PPF, EPF, bonds, and fixed deposits to provide stability.
- **Alternative Investments:** Diversify into cryptocurrencies, commodities, and international markets to balance risk.

Step C: Creating Multiple Income Streams

Diversifying your income ensures financial resilience. Robert G. Allen, in *"Multiple Streams of Income,"* underscores that diversified income sources are key to lasting financial security.

- **Side Businesses:** Create and monetize digital products, coaching programs, and online platforms.
- **Freelance Consulting:** Expand visibility through personal branding on digital marketplaces.
- **Content Creation:** Build passive income streams through blogs, podcasts, and social media channels.
- **Asset-Based Income:** Generate revenue from rental properties and leased assets.
- **Dividend Strategies:** Regularly invest in dividend-yielding stocks to maintain consistent passive income.

Step D: Settling Down and Family Planning

Choosing the right life partner and planning parenthood strategically are crucial to long-term success. Thomas

Stanley, in *"The Millionaire Next Door,"* highlights the strong correlation between stable, supportive relationships and wealth accumulation.

- **Selecting a Supportive Partner:** Prioritize compatibility, shared financial and career goals, and mutual respect to build a stable foundation.
- **Optimal Family Timing:** Research consistently shows late 20s and early 30s as ideal for starting a family, combining financial readiness with emotional maturity.
- **Family Financial Planning:** Budget proactively for child-related expenses, including education, healthcare, and lifestyle choices, ensuring that children become assets rather than financial liabilities.
- **Relationship Management:** Foster emotional intelligence, open communication, joint financial planning, and mutual support to ensure long-term relational success.

Social Proof & Learning from Experts

The strategies presented are reinforced by insights from leading experts:

- **Naval Ravikant,** *"The Almanack of Naval Ravikant":* Advocates specialized skills for exponential financial growth.

- **Robert Kiyosaki,** *"Rich Dad's Cashflow Quadrant":* Highlights passive income and strategic investing as foundational to wealth building.
- **Robert G. Allen,** *"Multiple Streams of Income":* Stresses income diversification for lasting financial stability.
- **Thomas Stanley,** *"The Millionaire Next Door":* Demonstrates the significant link between stable, supportive relationships and enduring wealth creation.
- **John Gray,** *"Men Are from Mars, Women Are from Venus":* Offers valuable insights into effective relationship management and communication—key factors for successful long-term partnerships.

Final Thoughts

For young Indian professionals aged 26 to 33, these transformative years offer unparalleled opportunities to achieve financial independence, career success, and profound personal fulfilment. Avoiding lifestyle inflation, focusing on strategic financial planning, and nurturing a supportive family environment are crucial. Choosing the right partner, strategic family planning, and diversifying income streams not only guarantee financial security but ensure meaningful, balanced lives that thrive beyond financial prosperity alone. **By strategically implementing these clear steps, young professionals can effectively escape the middle-class trap, build enduring wealth, and create a life that truly reflects their highest aspirations**

and deepest values.

Ages 33–40 | Securing Financial Independence, Time Freedom, and Creating Legacy

By the time an individual reaches their mid-30s, financial priorities shift from aggressive wealth accumulation to sustainable financial security and time independence. This is the stage where one must start **reaping the benefits of years of disciplined financial planning** while ensuring a stable and stress-free future. The late 30s are **not about working harder but working smarter,** with a focus on leveraging wealth, reducing dependency on active income, and securing generational assets.

For the **Indian middle class,** this phase is often filled with financial burdens—children's education, home loans, and lifestyle upgrades. However, those who have followed a structured approach to wealth-building in their 20s and early 30s will find that financial independence is **not a dream but an achievable reality.** The key is **passive income mastery, strategic wealth protection,** and ensuring that money continues to grow while requiring less active work.

Who?

This chapter is for individuals seeking financial freedom, **wanting to reduce dependency on active work while ensuring continuous financial growth.** Whether employed, running a business, or practicing a profession, the goal is to **transition from working for money to letting money work for you.**

Why?

The late 30s are a crucial **inflection point** where financial stability must be **secured for the long term.** According to a report by the **Reserve Bank of India,** over 70% of Indians continue working into their 50s and 60s **out of necessity rather than choice,** often because of poor financial planning.

By focusing on **high-yield investments, reducing reliance on active work, and setting up a legacy,** individuals can ensure that they are not caught in the **middle-class trap of constant financial stress.** Instead, they can begin enjoying the rewards of their hard work by gaining **time freedom**—the ability to do what they love, spend time with family, travel, or mentor the next generation.

What?

Achieving financial freedom before 40 is **not about retiring early, but about having the choice to work on your terms.** This phase focuses on three major objectives:

- **Scaling Passive Income** – Creating investments that generate **consistent, high-yield passive earnings.**
- **Reducing Active Work Dependency** – Structuring finances in a way that allows a **gradual reduction of active work hours** while income remains stable or grows.
- **Legacy & Wealth Protection** – Ensuring wealth **lasts beyond a single lifetime**, benefiting family and future generations.

Where?

This stage of life requires managing wealth through **investment portfolios, strategic estate planning, and transitioning into mentorship roles.** Financial success must be **sustained through diversified assets, business structures, and a well-protected financial framework.**

When?

Between **33 and 40**, individuals should focus on:

- **Ages 33–35:** Scaling investments and setting up long-term passive income structures.
- **Ages 36–38:** Gradually reducing active work and shifting toward wealth protection.

- **Ages 39–40:** Legacy planning, mentoring, and securing financial independence for the next generation.

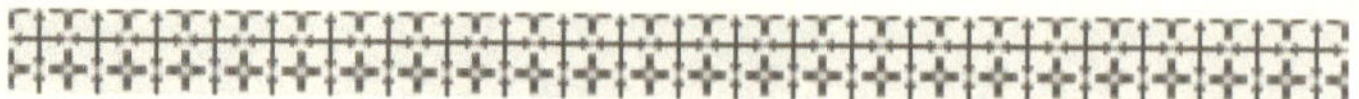

Perspective View

Growing up in a typical Indian middle-class family, financial security meant stability—a steady paycheck, saving diligently, and meticulously planning for predictable milestones like education, marriage, and home ownership. My parents worked tirelessly, managing their limited resources carefully to ensure we never went without essentials. Yet, despite their discipline and dedication, I noticed how they remained trapped in the cycle of earning, spending, and saving without truly experiencing financial freedom. Watching this cycle, I realized early in life that simply working harder wasn't enough; genuine prosperity required working smarter, strategically building wealth that grows independently, and ultimately liberating ourselves from constant financial stress. By the time I reached my mid-thirties, this understanding evolved into a clear vision: it wasn't just about accumulating wealth but about transitioning into a life defined by financial independence, time freedom, and meaningful legacy.

The years from age 33 to 40 represent a critical period where priorities shift from aggressive wealth accumulation towards leveraging accumulated wealth effectively. At this stage, Indian professionals often find themselves navigating responsibilities such as children's education, home loan repayments, and lifestyle enhancements. Without strategic planning, these financial pressures can overwhelm even high earners, trapping them in ongoing dependency on active income. However, having personally experienced and observed this challenge within my own community, I understood that those who planned strategically from their twenties and early thirties were able to face these obligations without stress. They had wisely built a robust foundation through diversified passive income streams, ensuring their money worked independently of their active efforts.

One of the key realizations during my journey was the importance of passive income mastery. Inspired by Abhishek Kumar's book The Richest Engineer, I learned that true financial independence occurs when passive earnings consistently surpass active income. In practical terms, this meant building a portfolio of dividend-yielding stocks and mutual funds, investing in rental properties, and creating digital products that generated consistent revenue without continuous effort. By carefully selecting and nurturing these passive streams, I reduced my reliance on a traditional career. Each stream—be it dividends, real estate rentals, or automated online businesses—formed a crucial pillar supporting financial independence, allowing me greater freedom to explore personal passions, spend quality time with family, and pursue meaningful projects without financial anxiety.

As I approached my late thirties, reducing active work dependency became essential—not necessarily to retire early, but to work selectively and on my own terms. Drawing lessons from Hector Garcia's Ikigai, I understood that a fulfilling life goes beyond financial security, encompassing purpose, passion, and balance. Prioritizing time over mere income became a guiding principle. I consciously moved away from high-stress environments, toxic workplace politics, and overly demanding professional commitments. Instead, I streamlined my responsibilities, choosing strategic engagements that leveraged my highest-value skills and interests, ensuring income continuity without excessive workload. I learned to delegate effectively, outsourcing operational tasks, automating business functions, and building efficient teams, thereby significantly freeing up my personal time. This approach not only enhanced my productivity but also boosted my overall life satisfaction and happiness, affirming the findings of the Harvard Business Review, which emphasize that individuals prioritizing time over monetary compensation enjoy greater long-term success and contentment.

Protecting wealth and preparing a legacy were equally critical in this phase. Growing up, I had witnessed friends and relatives whose families struggled after unforeseen tragedies, simply because they lacked structured estate planning. Determined not to repeat this mistake, I embraced comprehensive financial protection strategies early on. Utilizing insights from Robin Sharma's profound narrative, The Monk Who Sold His Ferrari, I learned that true prosperity is about lasting impact rather than temporary wealth. To safeguard this prosperity, I structured detailed estate plans, established trusts, acquired appropriate insurance coverage, and proactively educated my family about financial management. This preparation ensured a smooth transfer of assets without unnecessary legal complications or familial disputes.

Furthermore, conscious financial education for the next generation became a priority. From personal experience, I recognized that generational wealth often dissipates quickly due to poor financial literacy. Guided by insights from Forbes India, I ensured my children understood budgeting, investing, and responsible spending from an early age. This education was complemented by practical exposure to financial management, investments, and real-life decision-making processes. My aim was simple: empower my family not only to preserve the wealth we had created but also to grow it independently, ensuring it sustained beyond just one generation.

Creating a meaningful legacy extended beyond family alone. With financial independence, I dedicated significant effort toward mentoring younger professionals, sharing my experiences, mistakes, and lessons. Giving back to the community became a crucial element of my legacy planning. Philanthropic activities, social investments, and educational initiatives formed core components of my long-term strategy, ensuring my impact transcended financial measures alone. Wealth, as I learned, had the greatest value when utilized as a tool for positive social change and community enrichment.

Reflecting on this transformative phase, I understood that achieving financial freedom before 40 was not merely a personal milestone but a holistic transformation impacting every aspect of my life. It involved strategically leveraging professional growth, building diversified passive income streams, reducing active work dependency, and meticulously planning for wealth protection and legacy creation. The wisdom of financial experts like Abhishek Kumar, Hector Garcia, Robin Sharma, and institutions such as the Harvard Business Review, guided my approach, providing crucial frameworks for informed decisions. Ultimately, this phase of life was about redefining success—shifting away from traditional notions of endless accumulation and toward sustainable financial independence, time autonomy, and meaningful impact.

Today, I view the period from 33 to 40 not just as years of financial accomplishment but as transformative years that reshaped my life's trajectory. Achieving financial freedom empowered me to engage deeply with what truly mattered—family, personal growth, and societal contribution—without the limitations of financial constraints. The journey, although challenging, proved that strategic financial planning and disciplined execution could indeed transform dreams of independence into tangible realities. This realization stands as proof for every middle-class Indian striving for financial freedom; it is not merely possible but entirely achievable with deliberate planning and disciplined action.

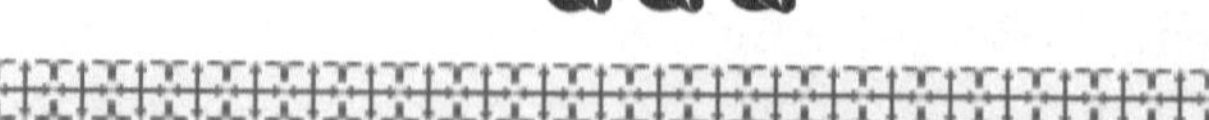

Implementation of the Concept

Step A: Building High-Yield Passive Income Streams

By this phase, income should **not solely depend on a job or business. The Richest Engineer** by Abhishek Kumar highlights how **passive income can surpass active income** if structured effectively.

- **Dividend Investments:** Creating a portfolio of dividend-yielding stocks and mutual funds that provide **steady cash flow.**
- **Real Estate Income:** Owning **rental properties or commercial spaces** that generate monthly passive earnings.
- **Business Automation:** If running a business, **automating operations and delegating management** to free up personal time.
- **Digital Assets:** Creating and monetizing **content, online courses, e-books, and intellectual property** that generate passive revenue.
- **Franchise or Licensing Models:** Expanding income streams by **licensing business models, franchising expertise, or revenue-sharing models.**

A report by **Knight Frank India** suggests that **real estate and dividend income** remain two of the most effective passive income generators for Indian professionals. Smart individuals will use this period to **expand these revenue sources while minimizing personal involvement.**

Step B: Reducing Active Work Hours While Maintaining Financial Growth

Financial freedom is not about quitting work entirely but about **having the flexibility to work by choice rather than obligation. Ikigai** by Hector Garcia emphasizes the importance of finding **fulfilment beyond just financial success.**

- **Prioritizing Time Over Money:** Recognizing that time is the most valuable resource and structuring life around **what truly matters.**
- **Selective Professional Engagement:** Moving away from **time-intensive jobs or business models** and focusing on high-value, strategic work.
- **Creating a Lean Lifestyle:** Financial security doesn't mean spending more; it means **spending wisely on experiences, health, and quality of life.**
- **Delegating & Outsourcing:** Hiring employees, delegating business functions, and **automating financial operations.**
- **Exiting High-Stress Environments:** Stepping away from **toxic work environments, high-pressure careers, and demanding clients** to maintain mental and emotional well-being.

A study by the **Harvard Business Review** found that professionals who prioritize time over money are **happier, more productive, and financially more successful in the long run.** The key is to **strategically exit time-consuming activities while ensuring income streams remain strong.**

Step C: Securing Financial Legacy Through Smart Estate Planning

Legacy building is about ensuring that **wealth is preserved and passed on efficiently. The Monk Who Sold His Ferrari** by Robin Sharma discusses how **true wealth is not just financial but also about creating a lasting impact.**

- **Estate & Will Planning:** Ensuring that wealth **transfers smoothly** to family members without legal complications.

- **Trusts & Wealth Protection:** Using **trust funds, life insurance, and family investment structures** to safeguard assets.
- **Financial Education for Family:** Teaching **children and dependents** about responsible wealth management to maintain financial security across generations.
- **Philanthropy & Giving Back:** Allocating a portion of wealth for **social causes, community development, or charitable activities** to leave a meaningful legacy.
- **Mentorship & Knowledge Sharing:** Using financial freedom to **mentor younger professionals, guide family members, and contribute to society.**

A study by **Forbes India** found that **most generational wealth disappears within two generations** due to poor financial education and mismanagement. Ensuring that **wealth serves its intended purpose** is crucial.

Social Proof & Learning from Experts

The principles in this chapter align with insights from financial experts and life mentors:

- **Abhishek Kumar,** *The Richest Engineer*: Explains how professionals can **build wealth beyond their salaries.**
- **Hector Garcia,** *Ikigai*: Highlights the importance of **fulfilment and purpose beyond money.**

- **Robin Sharma, *The Monk Who Sold His Ferrari*:** Redefines **true wealth as a combination of financial success, time freedom, and life impact.**

Final Thoughts

The **33–40 phase** is about **transitioning from an earning mindset to a financial independence mindset.** It is about ensuring that wealth continues to grow while work hours **gradually decrease,** allowing for a **life of choice rather than obligation.**

Individuals who implement **high-yield passive income strategies, reduce dependency on active work, and plan their financial legacy early** will experience a **lifetime of financial security and freedom.** The goal is not just about accumulating wealth but about achieving the **luxury of time—spending it with family, pursuing passions, and leaving a lasting legacy.**

Financial freedom before 40 is **not a fantasy—it is a result of strategic planning, disciplined investing, and a shift from active work dependency to wealth leverage.** Those who master this will **design a life of abundance, purpose, and long-term stability.**

Epilogue

The Journey Beyond 40 – Wealth, Freedom, and Legacy

By the time you reach 40, something shifts. The ambitions of your 20s—chasing stability, proving yourself, accumulating wealth—begin to evolve. You start to question whether you want to keep running the same race. You wonder if the wealth you've built is truly serving you or if you're still a prisoner to your work. The years of hustle, growth, and financial discipline should now lead to something greater: **time freedom, purpose, and legacy.**

If you've followed the roadmap laid out in this book, by now, you should have achieved what most middle-class working Indian professionals never do—**financial independence before 40.** Your income is no longer tied entirely to your job. You have **multiple streams of revenue**, and your investments generate passive returns. You are no longer working just to pay bills; your money is working for you. **You have choices.** And in this, lies true wealth.

The End of Financial Struggle – The Beginning of Real Life

For years, you chased financial security. You optimized earnings, built your career, invested wisely, and established multiple sources of income. But what comes next?

Financial freedom does not mean the end of work—it means **the freedom to choose what kind of work you do.** Whether you continue in your profession, grow your business, mentor others, or dedicate time to passion projects, the key shift is that you now work **because you want to, not because you have to.**

This is what separates those who planned early from those who didn't. While your peers are still stuck in the 9-to-5 cycle, worried about promotions, inflation, and EMIs, you have the privilege of focusing on the next phase—**building a lasting legacy.**

The Role of Architecture in My Journey

Looking back, I realize that my training as an **architect** gave me the biggest advantage in this process. Architecture is not just about designing buildings—it's about creating systems, foreseeing challenges, and executing solutions step by step. This structured approach is exactly what I applied to financial freedom.

An architect doesn't just draw sketches; he envisions the full structure before it is built. He accounts for foundations, materials, and future expansion. Similarly, I **designed my financial future** with precision. I treated income, investments, and passive revenue streams as different pillars of a well-structured life, ensuring that no single setback could collapse the entire system.

Moreover, architecture instilled in me an **entrepreneurial mind-set.** Unlike conventional professions, an architect **creates his own opportunities.** There is no fixed salary, no pre-defined career trajectory. You learn to **monetize your skills, build networks, and think like a business owner.** This perspective helped me escape the middle-class trap early.

Whatever your profession, you must think **beyond a paycheck.** You must **design your financial future** just like an architect designs a building—**with foresight, precision, and long-term vision.**

The Legacy Mind-set – What You Leave Behind

True financial success is not measured by your net worth alone, but by what you leave behind.

The final stage of wealth creation is **legacy building**—ensuring that your financial systems continue to generate prosperity beyond your lifetime. This means:

- **Estate Planning**: Drafting a will, setting up trusts, and ensuring that wealth is passed on efficiently.
- **Generational Wealth Education**: Teaching your children and heirs how to manage, grow, and sustain financial assets.
- **Mentorship & Knowledge Sharing**: Using your financial independence to mentor younger professionals, help others break free from the middle-class struggle, and contribute to society.
- **Philanthropy**: Giving back—whether through donations, impact investing, or community work—because wealth should also create positive change.

What Happens After 40?

By this stage, you have achieved financial and time freedom. What do you do next?

1. **Redefine Work** – Focus on passion-driven projects,

advisory roles, or purpose-driven work.

2. **Expand Your Investments** – Continue scaling your passive income sources, ensuring they remain optimized and profitable.

3. **Prioritize Health & Well-Being** – Now that money is no longer a daily stressor, invest in your physical and mental well-being.

4. **Travel, Explore, Experience** – Use your time freedom to travel, learn new skills, and enrich your life beyond work.

5. **Teach & Mentor** – The best way to solidify your wealth and knowledge is to pass it on. Whether through formal mentorship, online content, or simply guiding younger professionals, helping others navigate financial independence creates lasting impact.

Final Words – The Roadmap to Freedom

The greatest regret people have is **wishing they had started earlier.** Financial freedom is not about sudden windfalls or overnight success—it is about starting early, staying consistent, and designing your future with intention.

If you follow the roadmap in this book, by 40, you will not just be financially stable—you will be financially free. Free to live life on your terms, free to prioritize your family and passions, free to never worry about money again.

Most people spend their lives working for money. Few learn to make money work for them.

""Two roads diverged in a yellow wood""

Which path will you choose?

References & Further Reading

This section lists all the books, studies, and additional resources referenced throughout this book. These materials have been carefully selected for their relevance to financial independence, career growth, personal development, and wealth-building strategies. Readers are encouraged to explore these books to gain deeper insights into the principles and strategies discussed in this book.

1. Financial Education & Wealth Building

- **The Psychology of Money** – Morgan Housel (Understanding financial behaviour and money mindset)
- **Rich Dad Poor Dad** – Robert Kiyosaki (Shifting from a salary-dependent mindset to wealth-building)
- **The Richest Man in Babylon** – George S. Clason (Timeless financial wisdom and wealth-building strategies)
- **The Millionaire Fastlane** – MJ DeMarco (How to accelerate financial independence beyond a job)
- **The Dhandho Investor** – Mohnish Pabrai (Indian insights into value investing and risk management)
- **Rich Dad's Cashflow Quadrant** – Robert Kiyosaki (Transitioning from employee to investor mindset)
- **One Up on Wall Street** – Peter Lynch (Investment strategies for long-term financial security)

2. Career Development & Skill Mastery

- **So Good They Can't Ignore You** – Cal Newport (Why skills matter more than passion)
- **Deep Work** – Cal Newport (Mastering focus and high-value skills for career success)
- The 4-Hour Workweek – Tim Ferriss (Optimizing career and income streams for time freedom)
- **You Can Win** – Shiv Khera (Practical career success and self-motivation for Indians)
- **The Almanack of Naval Ravikant** – Naval Ravikant (Wealth-building and leverage principles)
- **The Defining Decade** – Meg Jay (Importance of strategic life decisions in your 20s)

3. Entrepreneurship & Alternative Income Streams

- The Lean Startup – Eric Ries (How to start and scale businesses with minimal risk)
- **Crushing It!** – Gary Vaynerchuk (Leveraging digital platforms for business and personal branding)
- **The $100 Startup** – Chris Guillebeau (Creating a sustainable business with low capital)
- **The Richest Engineer** – Abhishek Kumar (Indian perspective on wealth-building through engineering and business)
- **Multiple Streams of Income** – Robert G. Allen (Importance of income diversification)

4. Money Management & Investment Strategies

- **The Intelligent Investor** – Benjamin Graham (Value investing principles for financial security)
- **The Little Book That Still Beats the Market** – Joel Greenblatt (Simple yet effective investment strategies)
- **Unshakeable** – Tony Robbins (How to protect and grow wealth in volatile markets)
- **Common Stocks and Uncommon Profits** – Philip Fisher (Fundamentals of stock market investing)

5. Relationship Management & Emotional Intelligence

- **Men Are from Mars, Women Are from Venus** – John Gray (Insights into relationship dynamics and emotional intelligence)
- **The Millionaire Next Door** – Thomas Stanley (Correlation between stable relationships and wealth creation)

6. Parenting, Mindset & Early Financial Education

- **Brain Rules for Baby** – John Medina (How early childhood brain development impacts success)

- **The Whole-Brain Child** – Daniel J. Siegel & Tina Payne Bryson (Understanding emotional and cognitive development in children)
- **How Children Succeed** – Paul Tough (Role of resilience, curiosity, and character in early years)
- **Rich Dad Poor Dad for Teens** – Robert Kiyosaki (Introduction to financial literacy for young minds)
- **The 7 Habits of Highly Effective Families** – Stephen R. Covey (Building strong values and habits in children)

7. *Work-Life Balance, Productivity & Fulfilment*

- **Ikigai** – Hector Garcia & Francesc Miralles (Finding meaning and fulfilment in life and work)
- **Atomic Habits** – James Clear (Why habits matter more than goals in long-term success)
- **The 5 AM Club** – Robin Sharma (Building discipline and a productive routine)
- **The Subtle Art of Not Giving a F*ck** – Mark Manson (Prioritizing what truly matters in life)
- **The Monk Who Sold His Ferrari** – Robin Sharma (Shifting focus from wealth accumulation to life fulfilment)

Additional Reports & Studies Referenced

- Cambridge University Study on Financial Habits in Children

- Harvard Grant Study on Long-Term Happiness
- Reserve Bank of India Report on Middle-Class Financial Struggles
- Economic Policy Institute Study on Salary Growth
- Knight Frank India Report on Passive Income
- McKinsey & Co. Report on Career Growth
- National Bureau of Economic Research Study on Peer Influence
- Harvard Business Review Study on Time vs. Money Prioritization

This reading list is not exhaustive but provides a solid foundation for anyone looking to expand their knowledge in financial literacy, career development, entrepreneurship, and personal fulfilment. Each of these books and studies has contributed to the framework of this book, ensuring the strategies outlined are based on proven research and real-world applications. By diving deeper into these resources, readers can continue their journey toward financial freedom, time independence, and long-term success beyond the principles outlined in this book.

Happy Reading!

www.ingramcontent.com/pod-product-compliance
Lightning Source LLC
Chambersburg PA
CBHW062233150726
47991CB00006B/2559